For someone who wants to be someone

F#ck Your Sh*t

GET 1% BETTER EVERY DAY

To my parents and family

&

Special thanks, Saniya

F#CK YOUR SH*T

DARE TO LOSE. LEARN TO WIN.
THE WAY TO GET BETTER.

SHAILESH BHAT

It's you who you choose to be.

– Shailesh Bhat

Contents

Prologue

6ᵗʰ January 2025,

It is almost 11 o'clock at night and people out there are enjoying and having fun. I am sitting in my room alone after an exhausting day with a random thought to start writing a book that I have been trying to write for the past year. I don't know if this book will be published or just dumped in my recycle bin, yet I am trying to write. It's been a while since I read books just to understand how to write, improve my skills, and get better. For me, it feels very tough; every day, there is a relentless spirit inside me that does not settle for anything, and I think that is what is making me uneasy. For the past year, I have been in the same condition. It's just that I want to give it one shot, one try, because I feel there is 1% hope for everything; 1% to change, 1% to learn, and 1% for everything. If it's worth giving a shot, you should give it.

You see, nowadays, when my life goes simply and smoothly, I don't feel good. I realize that the ups and downs are the things that shape us, that make our life spicier and needed. So next time you get disappointed due to some obstacles or struggles, don't be disappointed. It's interesting; you just have to dive deep into it to understand the root cause and it's solved.

07th January 2025

If you look at where you are and where you have been, you can't figure out where you are going.

It was an exhausting day today. As I entered my room after coming back from college and finishing all the work, going to different brand showrooms and approaching them for work, and then I lay on my bed, it felt so relaxing. As I closed my eyes for seconds, I was asleep, but a few minutes later, I got up all of a sudden as I realized there was a lot of work to be done. There were many reasons for me to sleep, relax, and procrastinate, but there was one reason to get up and continue to work even though I was tired. I went and had a bath, had dinner, and came back to work at my desk. While working, I realized that there were many times I could have procrastinated and just enjoyed and had fun, but I had one reason to get up and work: the **WHY.**

I think "why" is one of the best motivators anyone could have in their life. That is what drives you, makes you do some crazy things, and gets you out of your comfort zone. If I didn't have a why, I wouldn't have been writing this book, starting an agency at 18, or trying out new things that excite me. Almost all the people I met told me not to take this risk or do a job for a while and then go for it, yet I am doing it because I have a why. My why is **"I don't want to settle for something else. I want to try it out, even if I fail. I am okay with it, but I want to try it out and at least I can. I TRIED AND I DID IT MY WAY."** For me, it's like even if I am alone, I will do it, *against all odds*, I will do it. All the people I have seen succeed or admire have one thing in common: a why. It is one of the things that drives a human being, and one who doesn't have a why, society gives him the why. It will take time for you or anyone to find the why, but once you have it, don't leave it. It's a good motivator. Let me tell my story of finding 'why'.

No One is Coming To Save You

I had just completed my 12th-grade exams during the pandemic, and I was at home exploring things. As usual, the story of every house, "Son, what are you going to do now? Doctor or Engineer?" situation arose. I was learning coding from YouTube and had completed one or two projects. As I did so, I felt overwhelmed and thought it was easy - what big rocket science in engineering! I told my parents I would be doing that, and my family was happy that our son would also be an engineer. I took admission for Artificial Intelligence and Data Science engineering at a college near my home. The initial 6 months, i.e., the 1st semester, were online due to COVID-19. After my semester ended in December, the next semester was offline, and we had to go to college. I was excited that I would finally be able to meet the friends with whom I had been chatting for the past six months, interact with my faculty one-on-one, join clubs in our college, and enjoy. Soon, the day came, and it was my first day in college. I went, interacted with my faculty, had fun with my new friends, enrolled in the sports club for football, and left for my home. On my way back, I had to walk a kilometer and then catch a bus to the nearest bus stop to my home. It took me approximately 15 to 20 minutes to reach home; I used to put on earphones and listen to songs on my way back home. Initially, the days were good, and I was having fun. I enrolled in some hackathons and also for incubation cells, as I always wanted to try startups because that excited me. Almost three to four months passed, and I was looking for internships and someone who could help me start my AI tech startup. I came across a man on a website called startupschool.com. I initially contacted him, hopped on a few meetings, and he had a fintech startup and was looking for a co-founder and tech guy. I worked with him for 2 – 3 weeks without telling my parents. One day, he told me he would hire me as his tech lead, and if everything went well, he would make me a co-founder. As it was my first time and I didn't have much experience, I was overwhelmed and I told my parents. They advised me to take it slow, but I continued working with him for the next 2 weeks. Then, one day, Dad told me it might be a trap, that he would use me and then leave. Dad used his sources to find out everything about that startup. In the end, I was advised to drop that idea and focus on my studies. At that time, I felt sad, my hopes were shattered, and I didn't know what to do. A few months later, I dropped out of engineering and pursued design as a career. During that period, I went through a lot of things; my mind was fucked up, I went to doctors, took medicines, and for me, it was horrible, but it was the turning point of my life. Everything happens for a reason, they say, and due to that startup, my interest in UI/UX grew more, and that excited me. But I was still confused about whether I should pursue it or not. Eventually, I chose design as a career and ended up at the same university, on the same campus, but in a design college building. Initially, I was a bit nervous as there was a fear of going back to the same place I had left behind, meeting my old friends, and facing them. Soon, my design course started, and I began going to college. A few months passed, I made new friends, started engaging in events and activities, and everything was going well. I started getting exposed to new things and learning, and that is where I found my why.

When I see myself 2 or 3 years behind, I realize what happened for good. I left engineering and joined design. That experience of a startup, dealing with people, and everything helped me, and that is why I have my reason to keep going: my why. There are stories and reasons in everyone's life due to which everyone gets their why reason to keep going. We just have to look for it and remember that everything happens for a reason. In a long-term view, everything happening now is always on our side, and there's a reason for it.

This book is about the same: my personal experiences and what I changed in myself that helped me change.

"You can't connect dots looking forward; you have to connect them looking backward."
— Steve Jobs

You grow when you know you have nothing to lose.

Wake the F#ck Up

"You can't connect dots looking forward, you have to connect them looking backward."
— Steve Jobs

What stage of life are you in?

Most of them don't know the answer to this, and I didn't either until a year ago. One day, while lying in bed and idly browsing Instagram while watching movies, I suddenly realized what I was doing. I had just gotten home from college and was browsing social media.

No professional aspirations.

Not fit.

No appropriate way of existence.

Then, I understood that everyone else was the same and that this was simply not me. The majority of people on the planet have put their lives on autopilot and are only surviving rather than experiencing them. All of us, myself included, wake up, go through the same routines, encounter the same difficulties, and gripe about the same issues.

Why?

Because it feels overwhelming to think of changing our lives. We keep thinking, "I'm going to have this, I'm going on a world tour, I'm going to concerts," but in reality, we never even begin because we believe that success will take a lot of work. That is incorrect.

When you conduct your life in a way that leaves no regrets at the end, you are truly successful. It's about learning, growing, and being able to impart your knowledge to others so they can grow even more and avoid the mistakes you made. Helping others rise is also a form of achievement.

The top 1% is distinguished from the others by their philosophy and outlook on life. I was at my lowest, and I believed that getting approval from others was the key to success.

However, I've discovered that it's far deeper as a result of my adventure. There is one prerequisite for success.

"YOURSELF, it demands you to change, you to think differently, you to get out of your comfort zone."

There was a man who failed and yet he was successful.

Sometimes, trying is enough because you reach a better place in the end.

Chapter 2

Just Get Going

---

*"Stop being afraid of what could go wrong and
start being excited about what could go right."*
– Tony Robbins

A lot of individuals hold off on starting until the "perfect" time. They believe, "I need to fix things first, then I'll start, because I'm too messed up right now." The sad reality is that if you keep waiting for things to go exactly as planned, you will never get started. In actuality, the appropriate moment is always right now; there is no such thing as a perfect moment. Repeating to yourself, "I'll clean up this mess first and then start," will keep you caught in a never-ending cycle of putting things off.

Begin sloppy; begin before you're prepared. Accept the process and begin with the mess. Because you're only slowing down your development while you wait for things to fall into place. There is never a bad time to start.

It's okay if you don't know where to begin; just make a goal. I'm not referring to some lofty, ambitious objective. I'm referring to modest, doable objectives. One step at a time, please. Deciding to make today productive and win your day could be the first step.

In a well-known speech, Admiral McRaven discusses the importance of *"making your bed"* as the first thing you should do in the morning. It looks easy, doesn't it? However, one little deed establishes the tone for the remainder of your day. Making your bed is a victory because it's a quick, easy chore that you can get done right away. No matter how minor, it makes you feel proud and accomplished. The next duty and challenge follow this little victory, and before you realize it, you're in the thick of things.

Therefore, even in the simplest ways throughout the day, start small. Whether it's writing a single line, getting out of bed early, or finishing one worthwhile activity, increase that momentum.

You'll quickly be on your way once one minor victory leads to another.

"Perfectionism is a disease.
Procrastination is a disease.
ACTION is the cure."
– Richie Norton

Perfectionism Sucks.

The sickness of perfection is terrible; I spent about a year and a half attempting to write a flawless book, yet even if I wait another ten years, it will still be flawed. Because someone takes the time to pay attention to small details, beautiful things exist. The world wouldn't be as wonderful without perfection. Everything around us would be of poor quality. Both the world's imperfections and its perfection make it attractive.

Steve Jobs was likewise insanely detail-oriented. Even though no one would be able to see the inside of the first Macintosh computer since only a technician with specialized tools could open it, he insisted that the circuit board cables be neat and straight when building the computer. Don't make being a perfectionist your default setting. Adapt it to the situation. Don't use perfection to cover up your indolence. A task that can be completed in a few minutes cannot be left undone for days.

"Things done are more important than things done perfectly."

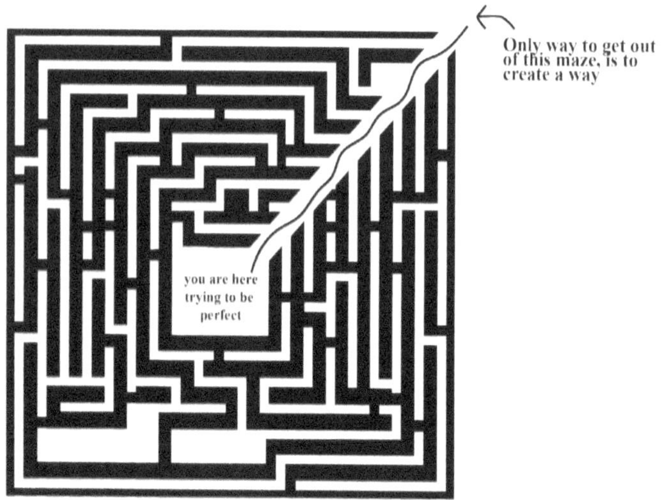

What's in your hand?

It's important to concentrate just on your controllable aspects. Even though we frequently hear advice on how to deal with difficult situations, the constant barrage of information we are exposed to on a daily basis tends to overpower these helpful reminders. The majority of this information is pointless, and worse, it diverts our attention from the important things.

For instance, this morning, I came across a story concerning the media industry when I opened Google to see what the most recent news was. I spent thirty minutes dumb-scrolling through reels on Instagram as a result of it. I lost valuable time that I will never get back in an instant. Does that sound familiar? We all start with one thing and end up doing something completely different and something we never planned to do.

Yes, it's good to be aware of the world, but let's face it: we can't possibly use all of the information we take in. The majority of it is noise, and it is frequently a huge waste of time to chase it. We waste hours watching TV series we don't particularly care about, following meaningless debates on Twitter, or browsing Instagram in an attempt to "kill time."

However, why "kill" something so valuable? We handle time as if it were limitless, even though it is the one resource we can never get back. We should be worried about how recklessly we waste our time, not about the insignificant things we see online.

From global news to social media drama, we feel compelled to react to everything we come across. The harsh reality is that *we have no control over the words or actions of others*. A recession, a war, a natural disaster, or a protest—there's always something to be concerned about. The negative things in the world are unavoidable, but you have power over how much of your energy you allow them to take up.

The secret is to learn to be unconcerned with things that are beyond your control. Learning to not allow them to control your happiness is more important than completely ignoring them.

Ask yourself: What makes you happy?

Simple things like close relationships, fulfilling employment, thought-provoking books, or a tranquil stroll in the outdoors are probably what it is.

> *"Circumstances don't make the man; they only reveal him to himself."*
> *— Epictetus*

Start with yourself, which you can control. Make an effort to make your life and the lives of people around you better. Making your life and the lives of others you care about better is itself a huge accomplishment; you don't need to change the entire world.

There will always be chaos and diversions in the world. However, avoid making life more difficult than necessary by squandering time on unimportant or uncontrollable things. Your life is shaped by how you spend the limited time you have. Make an informed decision.

You have enough resources to start, rest everything you get in the journey.

Just start.

Believe in
Great thing before
Great things happen

It takes time for things to happen; overnight success is a myth.

Chapter 3

The Mindset

---

*"If you can build a muscle, you can
build a mindset."*
— Jay Shetty

Inside your mind.

Similar to a muscle, your brain grows, develops, and changes based on incidents taking place in your life. Specific regions of the brain grow, along with the connections and individual neurons. Just like weights can build your bicep muscles, the brain can be trained to improve its functioning, which makes it tougher, smarter, and more powerful.

The body's building blocks, neurons, create intricate networks in order to transmit and interpret information. In response to one's behavior, thoughts, and knowledge, these relationships change. This demonstrates that your brain has the unique ability to rewire itself, making it an organ that is ever-evolving and not static.

Understanding that one's thoughts portray the shape of your world is the first step to controlling your mind. When looking back, have you ever made a decision that was puzzling? That is due to the fact that humans aren't as rational as we want to think we are. The majority of our actions and emotions stem from perceptions, which are deep-rooted in our thoughts.

You will begin to see the world from a negative perspective; for instance, if your head is full of negative thoughts. Your behavior, emotions, and even results start to center around that negativity. In essence, by looking for evidence to support your beliefs, your brain validates them. This is how we frequently invent our limitations and worries.

Conversely, there is a significant change when you surround yourself with empowering, upbeat thoughts. You start working toward something without even realizing it when you start to believe in it. Your brain learns to see indications, opportunities, and solutions that support those constructive views. You begin gathering information, making strategies, and acting to achieve your objective.

The power of the mind is shockingly basic, despite its tremendous complexity: what you feed it influences what it generates. Positive feedback encourages innovation, resilience, and advancement, but negative input produces negative results.

Knowing is the initial step. Understanding the depth of the nature of your mind's thoughts unlocks the predisposition to be able to change your perspectives and your life.

In the end, your brain is the most powerful tool that you will ever have. Manage it. Expand your mental faculties intentionally. Remind yourself that how you look at the world is exactly how it looks back at you.

Stress in a good way

Stress is nothing but a state of mind when you start thinking about future consequences that may not happen. It comes from overthinking and keeping expectations. Mainly, when you do the work which you don't like or are forced to do, your stress increases, because you never want that. Due to stress, many people seem older than their age. People nowadays have hectic lives and are in intense rivalry with one another almost all the time. Stress is the body's normal reaction to this extreme level of information that it perceives as potentially harmful or troublesome. In theory, this is a helpful response as it keeps us alive in dangerous environments.

Throughout our evolutionary history, humans have employed this reaction to our environment. We have utilized this reaction throughout our evolutionary history to deal with challenging circumstances and escape from predators. Our brain's neurons trigger the pituitary gland, which then releases hormones that cause the body to create corticotropin.

A playful life makes a stress-free life.

The sympathetic nervous system then distributes this hormone throughout the body. Subsequently, the adrenal gland is stimulated to secrete cortisol and adrenaline.

While cortisol boosts the production of dopamine and blood glucose, which is what gets us "charged up" and enables us to tackle difficulties, adrenaline increases our heart rate, breathing rate, and muscular contractions, readying the body to react to perceived threats. Therefore, even if taking on challenges keeps the mind and body alive, we need to modify our high-stress lives to prevent our bodies from aging too quickly.

**Be so rooted in yourself that
you have no time
to focus on useless sh*t.**

*One needs a higher ambition to live a certain way that
makes him/her stay focused.*

Chapter 4

Being Distracted

> *"What you stay focused on will grow."*
> *— Roy T. Bennett*

Trying to do too many things at once is harmful because it steals your energy and scatters your mind. It is possible to put stress and frustration upon yourself when you lose concentration and your mind decides to roam freely. Important objectives require attention; they should not be worked on with a low focus or performed half-heartedly.

Our minds do have their limits, and so does their deeply ingrained complexity. People tend to exaggerate what they can do, tackling problems until they get swamped and hardly accomplish anything. Trying to achieve everything single-handedly and then ultimately failing is something that I've done endlessly. A popular saying goes: "Jack of all trades, master of none." This saying hits differently and serves as a reminder that pursuing everything often means achieving nothing. Recently, during my vacations, I got the ultimate chance to do nothing. I could have gone out, watched movies, or even just strolled outside. But instead, I stayed ambitious, wrote this book, and expanded my design agency.

This was not an easy decision to make, but it was the most beneficial. It is my genuine belief that every individual deserves a job that is resonant, inspiring, stimulating, and most importantly, serves a purpose. This decision truly affirms that belief. When we are lost, when we are simply going through the motions or doing meaningless things, that is when the sense of fulfillment starts to fade. It is far more beneficial to devote your time and effort to something that truly matters and means the most to you rather than simply being busy for the sake of it.

No matter how busy the world may seem, there is always something you can do to pursue your goals or passions. For example, whenever I am free and have no plans, I utilize those hours to contribute to my book, sketch out ideas, or even study the latest trends in design. Having these sights set keeps me constantly motivated. Fitness junkies, for instance, can focus all of that energy elsewhere, like trying new workouts or improving their well-being.

For an artist, it could be the discovery of new art forms or techniques. Having a personal mission or aim that inspires you and provides direction for your life is crucial.

There's a sense of freedom in that because you eliminate outside noise and distractions, which enables you to take charge of your own achievement when you zone in on objectives that you can manage. You spend your energy on your passions and personal development instead of worrying about what you cannot change.

Instead of just thinking about getting work done, it is actually more about executing work that matters to you. It is in the chaos of life that you find meaning and clarity. With something substantial to focus on, your days aren't aimless anymore but rather purposeful, and that in itself is a step toward a successful and happy life.

*"Too many distractions lead to
a heavy mind."*
— Naval Ravikant

Work on the right things

You're wasting not just time, but also potential, if you're working on something that shouldn't have been done in the first place. Knowing what to work on and, just as importantly, what not to work on is one of the most crucial life lessons. One of the worst things you can do with your limited time is to spend it on things that don't fit with your mission or hobbies. You will inevitably put things off if you don't enjoy doing them. Humans tend to shy away from things that don't make us happy or resonate with us. Consider telling an artist to become an engineer. The artist would probably put off doing the job, avoid it, or do it only partially.

Why?

Because they are not destined to do that; it is not their calling. Their lack of desire will always hold them back, even if they are capable of doing it. This is why it's so important to do something that resonates with your innermost self. Before diving into any task or project,

Ask yourself: "Am I working on the right thing?"

This is a powerful question because it makes you consider whether your current work is in line with your long-term goals as well as passions. You should follow your passions, but keep in mind that even your favorite work will have difficult aspects. You can't completely avoid challenges; in fact, accepting them is a necessary part of the journey. Many people never pursue their passions because they are afraid or feel pressured to live up to others' expectations, and eventually, they come to regret their choice—or rather, the path they didn't choose. This is one of the most enduring types of disappointment.

It makes you feel the way that creates the "what ifs" and causes pain deep within. You feel like that because you have only been there. I did engineering before switching to design. Back then, to my parents and society, going through it was seemingly the "safe" and "right" decision. But I just felt in my heart that it wasn't for me. I was only doing everything to meet everyone else's expectations. I lacked the passion.

It was hard, but what needed to be done was that I made the decision to drop out and focus on something that made me happy: designing. I don't consider working on concepts and marketing materials as work anymore. In fact, it is one of the things that keeps me active, creative, and motivated. With every job I take on, it feels like I am one step closer to my life goal, and that feeling is priceless. It usually isn't easy, but that's always the case when you follow what you love. Regardless, any challenges I have faced have always been outweighed by the joy I feel after achieving what I love.

Life is too short to waste on things that don't excite you, and this is a clear lesson. *Discover what inspires you*, what makes you want to get out of bed in the morning, and what makes you want to give it your all. But acknowledge that there will be challenging and laborious times even in your passion.

Avoid being afraid of them. The journey is valuable because of the challenging aspects, which foster character, resilience, and a sense of accomplishment.

Therefore, consider this: *Are you working on the correct project?* It's time for a change if the response is negative. If you must, start small, but start. Because you stop just existing and begin to actually live when your actions are in line with your desires. At that point, life starts to have a purpose.

*Figure out
what's distracting you.*

Pomodoro Technique

This is one of the best techniques to eliminate distractions and increase productivity. To use this strategy, simply work for 25 minutes without interruptions, then take a 5-minute rest before repeating. If you are fully engaged in any work, you may have noticed that you stop.

Worrying about everything else causes you to lose track of time. It's rare, but when it happens, it brings joy. Finding joy requires engaging in enjoyable activities. You can't experience this if you dislike your employment. Loving your work is the only way to feel this.

Time is like holding sand in hand, the more you try, the more it slips out.

People who choose to work on their goals every day have much time, not the ones who lie in bed and think they have time.

Chapter 5

Time Feels Like Holding Sand in Hand

A year is made up of 8,760 hours, 525,600 minutes, and 31,536,000 seconds. However, some people use this time to develop, expand, and grow, while others let it pass them by, squandering chances and potential. Time is moving more quickly than we realize and doesn't wait for anyone. Before you know it, you're looking back and wondering where it all went. Days become months, and months become years. We don't have as much time as we believe, which is a reality that many of us choose to ignore. Life doesn't stop when we put things off or divert our attention to pointless pursuits. So, sit down for a while, somewhere quiet, by yourself, and really think.

Ask yourself: Am I using my time wisely?

Will I regret not doing the things I could have done when I look back on this moment? Because life is brief, you will undoubtedly look back on your decisions as you get older. The regret of not acting, of not following your interests, of allowing indolence or fear to hold you back—those are weighty emotions. Although time is our most precious resource, we waste it the most recklessly.

"We must use time as a tool, not as a couch."
— John F. Kennedy

The admonition to stop wasting time and do something productive is something we've all heard. However, we frequently ignore it, believing that we have plenty of time to begin tomorrow. Many people are stuck because of this delusion, the idea that there is always time. You'll wake up at seventy-one day and wish you had woken up sooner, not just from your bed, but from this delusion as well. You'll regret not spending that extra hour scrolling or binge-watching that web series and instead using that time to create something worthwhile. Your life will start to change the instant you quit blaming yourself and take action.

Buying a luxury car in six months or becoming a billionaire in a month are not the objectives. The true objective is considerably more straightforward but profound: to improve daily by simply 1%. Every day, set aside even an hour or two to work on anything that will help you achieve your goals. It's about taking steady, purposeful strides ahead rather than making big leaps. It doesn't simply go away when we put off doing the things we really need or want to do.

It remains in our thoughts, causing anxiety and serving as a subliminal reminder of our procrastination. We know deep down that we are capable of more, and that unfulfilled task or unachieved goal eats away at our peace. Every day counts.

Each hour matters.
Each moment matters.

**Wars are never won
in bed, you need
to go to the battlefield.**

*To be a butterfly and see the world's beauty, you have
to get out of the cocoon.*

Chapter 6

Comfort Zones

> *"Step outside your comfort zone because that's*
> *the only way you're going to grow."*
> *— Brewer*

It's incredibly easy to stay in bed, endlessly scrolling through Instagram or watching random YouTube videos that add no real value to your life. It feels effortless, doesn't it? But getting up every day at 6 a.m., shaking off the comfort of your sheets, and getting to work? That's hard. It's boring. It's uncomfortable. And yet, that's exactly where growth begins—outside your comfort zone.

The truth is that nothing meaningful happens automatically. Success doesn't magically knock on your door one day. You have to go out and chase it. Growth demands discomfort. It demands effort.

You have to face those early mornings and tough days, even when every fiber of your being just wants to stay where it's safe and easy. But here's the catch: when you start stepping out of your comfort zone, something magical happens. You start to change gradually. You begin to push yourself, wake up earlier, and take on new projects because it gives you a sense of success and purpose rather than because you have to.

It's your life. No one else is living it for you, and no one else's opinion should matter. Let them think whatever they want. Their judgments have nothing to do with your journey. You either step out, grow and make something of your life, or you stay in your comfort zone and live with regret.

And here's the thing about stepping out of that comfort zone: it's not a straight path. This is not a one-shot scenario when you try something new and everything just falls into place. It won't most of the time. You'll have to change, adapt, and keep going. An aspect of the process involves failure. You already know what will happen if you continue to be lazy; it will be the same as it has always been. But eventually, everything will make sense if you keep trying, exploring, and going forward.

Take this book, for example. The one you're holding is the 5th or 6th draft. It took me over a year and a half to get here. And even now, as you read it, I don't know what you'll think of it. I don't know how many copies will sell or how they'll be received. But here's what I do know: I tried. I stepped out of my comfort zone. I poured my energy into something I believed in. And that, in itself, is enough for me—because I know I won't regret it.

Elon Musk, for instance, is another excellent example. People made fun of him when he founded SpaceX. They informed him that a private corporation could not compete with NASA, much less develop rockets. Beyond the comfort of his previous success with PayPal, he was venturing into entirely unexplored ground. However, he was not deterred by the opinions of others or the dread of failing. His initial three rocket launches were a complete failure. Musk persisted when any reasonable person would have given up. He improved his strategy based on those setbacks, and SpaceX was successful by the fourth launch. That achievement wasn't a coincidence; rather, it came from persistently pushing himself beyond his comfort zone, overcoming obstacles, and never giving up.

Growth isn't easy, and it's never comfortable. But it's worth it. So, stop waiting for life to change on its own. Step out, try, fail, learn, and keep going because the only real failure is staying stuck where you are.

Freedom = Discomfort.

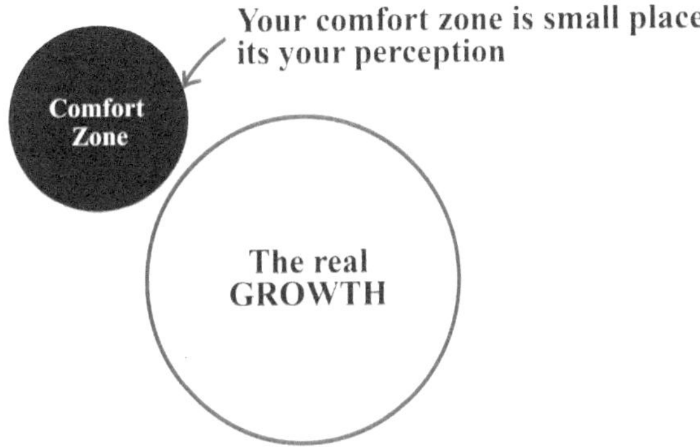

The regret of not trying will always hurt more than the discomfort of stepping out of your comfort zone.

Life is not like a highway straight and smooth, it's a road of twists and turns.

Life never goes as you planned; if it was so simple, anyone could have made it.

Chapter 7

Life is not Linear

"I don't believe that life is linear. I think of it as circles - concentric circles that connect."
— Michelle Williams

The key point to note is that wonderful things take time to occur due to the fact that they build up, and that takes time. Success does not occur overnight.

It sometimes takes a long time for things to take shape and transform, which, for the most part, does not happen all at once. If you find yourself in just one complicated mess, it is quite easy to feel trapped. It is only when you look at your path over a prolonged period, like weeks, months, or even years, that you realize your growth. For instance, when I take a look at some two or three years back, I feel like my perspective toward life, along with a lot of other areas, has changed and still has to change.

There are those dark moments too, when it looks like there are no paths ahead or where I need to go is very unclear. And that's when the best thing to do is re-evaluate and devise a new, explorable approach.

This isn't a defeat—it's a strategic pause. Accepting the need to retreat and recalibrate can be one of the most challenging things to do, but it's often necessary for long-term success. Setbacks aren't the end of the road; they're part of the process. Sadly, a lot of people allow these situations to depress them. Unaware that they are halfway up the mountain and cannot see the magnificent vista that lies just a little bit farther ahead, they give up.

Your vision is what sustains you. When things become challenging along the path, it is the drive that keeps you going.

The unattainable can become attainable with a compelling vision. It serves as your north star and guiding light, in addition to being a direction.

Vision transforms ordinary people into extraordinary achievers. Start with yourself: define who you are and what you stand for. Refine your personality. Choose your destination, articulate your goals, and let that vision fuel you through every twist, turn, and setback.

Read the narrative by J.K. Rowling. She experienced an astounding number of setbacks prior to becoming the well-known author of Harry Potter. Rowling was a single mother who battled depression and financial hardship. Her first novel was written in cafes, frequently after she had put her infant to sleep. Twelve publishers rejected her manuscript for Harry Potter and the Philosopher's Stone. After the first few rejections, let alone the twelfth, most individuals would have given up. Rowling, however, had an idea. She persisted because she had faith in her tale. After a while, Bloomsbury made the decision to risk her book, and the rest is history. Generations of readers have been inspired by her writings, which have sold over 500 million copies worldwide. Rowling's perseverance and foresight defined her, not her failures.

The wise words of Warren Buffett, "It takes 20 years to build a reputation and five minutes to destroy it," are related to this. The amount of work needed to develop, advance, and achieve success is enormous. However, development and advancement are considerably more potent than any setback. Growth is what overcomes all barriers, uncertainties, and difficulties. Even modest progress creates the momentum required to overcome obstacles that once seemed insurmountable.

Keep in mind that setbacks are not failures but rather stepping stones. They force you to adapt, get stronger, and find a better way. Even if the road to success may be challenging and complicated, the vision of what lies ahead makes the ascent worthwhile. Stay true to your vision no matter how difficult the path becomes. There is a view worth every ounce of effort on the other side of the fight, so let it be the fuel that gets you through the most difficult times.

If you start comparing,
to people, you, because
nothing in your eyes.

When you compare yourself, you decrease your value.

Chapter 8

Compare Yourself with Your Past.

<hr>

"Comparison is an act of violence against the self."
— Iyanla Vanzant

Have you ever looked at someone during your journey and thought:

I wish I had a life like theirs.

I wish I could achieve what they've achieved or perform better than them.

You're not alone, I assure you. At some point, everyone has thought of those things. This comparison is indeed one of the main causes of dissatisfaction. There will always be someone who seems better, more accomplished, or more successful than you, regardless of how good you are, how hard you work, or how many successes you have under your belt. It is unavoidable.

I doubt I would ever have the guts to write a book in my lifetime if I were to sit here and judge myself against well-known authors or more seasoned authors.

Why?

Because the scale of comparison is infinite and it never ends. There will always be someone with better prose, more refined storytelling, or a bigger audience. But the moment you let that define you, the moment you let someone else's journey overshadow your own, is the moment you lose. Instead of allowing comparison to immobilize you, focus on the things you can control, such as your work, your voice, and your personal growth. Here's a secret: you can create something meaningful without being the best. All you have to do is start, try, and continue.

Think of it this way: the billionaire doesn't care what people say about his business, his choices, or his lifestyle. He just gets up every day and works because that's what he has to do. His focus isn't on the noise around him; it's on his purpose, his craft. And that's how he succeeds—not by constantly looking sideways at others, but by looking straight ahead.

There's a voice inside all of us—a voice I like to call our "true self." It's the real you, the person you were before the noise of the world began shaping your thoughts. This authentic self does not compare or compete. It understands just what you desire, what motivates you, and what gives your life purpose. But it's also the voice that pushes you, critiques your poor attempts, and reminds you that you're capable of more. This mental discussion defines who we become. Sure, confronting this voice is uncomfortable, but it's vital. Without it, we would stagnate.

The reality is that failure and disappointment are the prices we pay for striving to improve. The world is tough, and not everyone gets a fair share of success. Winners don't take it all, but they take most. And the bottom? It's not a good place to be—I can tell you that from personal experience. The bottom is where people are stressed, unhappy, and drowning in self-doubt. It's where dreams suffocate under the weight of fear and inertia. People at the bottom often stop believing in themselves, and that's the cruelest thing of all. They listen to that self-deprecating voice in their head, the one that tells them they're not good enough, not capable, not worthy. They weave a story of failure around themselves and worst of all—they believe it.

But here's the good news: that doesn't have to be your story. The power to rewrite it lies in your hands. You don't have to be perfect; you just have to show up and keep trying.

Success isn't about avoiding failure; it's about persisting despite it. Start listening to your genuine self—not the voice of comparison or doubt, but the one that tells you what is most important to you.

Stop looking at what others have and instead focus on what you can produce. Because, at the end of the day, your path is yours alone, and the only way to live without regret is to make it truly yours.

Patience is just stubbornness.

When you keep patience with things you love, you indirectly refuse to give up on them.

Chapter 9

Long Runs

"Patience is a virtue, and I'm learning patience.
It's a tough lesson."
— Elon Musk

What is patience?

Patience, in my opinion, is a type of stubbornness for things you genuinely care about and support. It is the reluctance to give up, even when the odds appear to be stacked against you, and the belief that your efforts will eventually pay off. Patience is the quiet conviction that improvement does not happen overnight—it is developed over days, months, or even years of constant effort and unflinching hope.

The life of a farmer provides the best example of patience. When a farmer wishes to develop a crop, such as wheat, he or she does not just sow the seeds and collect the crop the next day.

The procedure begins with cultivating the land and preparing it for planting, followed by sowing the seeds and daily watering, caring, and safeguarding the plants. The farmer works with faith, knowing that every modest activity contributes to the final harvest. Similarly, anything essential and worthwhile in life demands the same level of patience. It's a process—a step-by-step trip that requires time, effort, and consideration.

> *Sometimes, things aren't clear right away.*
> *That's where you need to be patient and persevere*
> *and see where things lead.*
> *— Mary Pierce*

Every modest action, such as watering a field, may appear inconsequential at first, yet these efforts compound over time to produce remarkable outcomes. Patience encourages us to respect the process, believe in the journey, and find value in the modest progress we achieve. It develops our character, fortifies our determination, and teaches us resilience in the face of adversity. Setbacks and failures are not dead ends; rather, they serve as milestones on the way to achievement. Without patience, we risk giving up too soon and missing out on the benefits of persistence.

Patience is fundamentally an act of trust. It is the belief in the future while remaining entirely focused on the present. It is believing that the work you do now will provide the desired results tomorrow. Just as the farmer never doubts the viability of the seeds he sows, we must believe in the viability of our own efforts and goals.

Compounding effect: Every choice you make ignites, every step counts.

Whenever the path unfortunately appears never-ending and you feel like you are making little to no progress, keep in mind that true patience is not just sitting back and waiting. It is an active process that requires effort, faith, and attendance daily. This attribute involves perseverance while maintaining effortless strength, such as a farmer coaxing the barren land toward his desired state by constantly working on its needs and nurturing the relationship with the land that was once forlorn.

Follow your gut and intuitions; they take you to your destiny.

Fear only gives
your regrets.

If you can't leave your fear behind and start something, you will end up with regret.

Chapter 10

Fear of Fear

---

*"It is always easier to be afraid of something
you cannot see."
– Neil Gaiman*

What Is Fear?

We all experience fear, but the meaning and impact differ from person to person. For some, anxiety originates from the threat of failure—not attaining what they had imagined. This anxiousness frequently produces inflated expectations that are difficult to meet. For me, fear is simply an excuse not to try anything new.

Fear is natural, but staying in its shadow is an option. Fear can either drive you to strive harder or function as a barrier that hinders you from succeeding.

Personally, the fear of regret motivates me the most. I don't want to look back one day and say, "I wish I had tried."

Everyone faces different kinds of fears—fear of regret, fear of embarrassment, fear of failure—but one thing is certain: if you don't confront your fear, you'll never move forward. Fear only grows stronger when you avoid it.

The Fear of Failure

Fear of failure can be paralyzing. It may prevent you from attempting new things, taking risks, or pursuing progress because you are terrified of what might go wrong. People who strive for perfection typically suffer the most from this fear – they set unrealistically high goals for themselves and worry they won't live up to them.

The emotional effects of fearing failure can include:

- Avoidance
- Anxiety
- Losing self-control
- Feeling helpless

Rarely does an actual threat in front of us cause us to become engrossed in scared thoughts. Rather, our minds are deceiving us, frequently with the help of trauma or memories from the past. This fear-based thought pattern can keep us caught in a mental loop as we deal with one issue after another.

Overcoming Fear

Facing fear head-on is the only way to overcome it. Fear only gains strength when it is avoided. The secret is to change your perspective and convince yourself, "I'll deal with whatever comes up." You can free yourself from fear by accepting that failure or shame is not the end of the world.

I have firsthand knowledge of this. Being an introvert, I've always battled social anxiety, and I find speaking in front of an audience or even being at huge social gatherings terrifying. However, I am aware that I cannot let this dread permanently define who I am. One of the reasons I wrote this book is to push myself out of my comfort zone and confront my fear of being social. Writing is my way of breaking through that fear and saying, "I'll grow, no matter what."

Here's the truth: fear loses its grip the moment you accept it. When you stop resisting and say, *"Yes, I'm afraid, but I'll still move forward,"* fear begins to fade. It becomes a non-issue because you've robbed it of its power.

At the end of the day, fear is often just a product of our imagination—a shadow of a problem that feels bigger than it is. And once you face it, you'll realize it was never as strong as you thought.

So, don't let fear derail your life. Embrace it, confront it, and keep moving forward. Only then will you see that what once seemed impossible was just another step on your journey.

Fear of Regrets

Another method we show ourselves what we must do moving forward, rather than what we wish we could have done in the past, is through our fear of regret. The truth is that most individuals regret not doing anything more often than they regret doing something. This is not an accident. Regret isn't meant to make us feel awful about not living up to our standards. It is attempting to inspire us to meet our standards. It aims to inspire us to continue living up to them.

Do you regret telling yourself to do it right now?

Telling oneself that you should have put in more effort is regret.

Knowing that you had the opportunity to make better decisions is what regret is.

The legendary basketball player and businessman Magic Johnson joined the NBA at the age of 19 and began receiving endorsement deals. Even though he knew he wanted to negotiate with a sneaker manufacturer, he regretted not knowing enough about investing to consider accepting a stock transaction rather than a cash offer. He stated, "Converse came in and offered me some money." Phil Knight came into the room when Nike was only a year or two old.

He stated he would give me shares even if he didn't have much money. Johnson has given it a lot of thought since accepting the monetary offer from Converse. "Damn, did I do anything wrong?" he remarked, "I'm still kicking myself." "I get angry whenever I'm in a Nike store. Right now, I could have profited from everyone purchasing Nikes."

Fear of Embarrassment

Everyone fears embarrassment in social situations or anywhere else; if we do something incorrectly and others do not, we perform the work out of fear. When we realize that we did not act in a manner in which we are proud, we experience embarrassment. We can never be embarrassed by other people. You cease always feeling embarrassed when you genuinely and fully believe that you are doing the best you can with what is in front of you. People's criticism and remarks can only make you feel awful, but when we embrace who we are and keep going, we feel proud of ourselves.

The dark side of humiliation is shame. At this point, the normal emotion of embarrassment becomes a means for us to fully condemn ourselves as humans. This sensation pulls us into the shadows, where we begin experimenting and remain.

Overthinking only leads you to a messy place.

Even if you think 100 times about one situation, your action will define the outcome of that situation.

Chapter 11
Thinking vs. Overthinking

बन्धुरात्मात्मनस्तस्य येनात्मैवात्मना जितः |
अनात्मनस्तु शत्रुत्वे वर्ते तात्मैव शत्रुवत् || 6||

bandhur ātmātmanas tasya yenātmaivātmanā jitaḥ
anātmanas tu śhatrutve vartetātmaiva śhatru-vat

Translation

For those who have conquered the mind, it is their
friend. For those who have failed to do so, the mind
works like an enemy.

We talk about overthinking; I think I show it well. No matter what happens, I have this habit of making up scenarios in my mind—things that aren't true and likely won't occur. It's like my brain works overtime for no reason.

Overthinking is just the devil inside you.

Our thoughts serve as the foundation for all that we produce. We cannot feel anything without thought. It's vital to understand that thoughts are nouns, not something we do, but something we have. A thought requires no effort and occurs naturally. We also have no control over the thoughts that enter our minds. Thoughts originate from something beyond our conscious consciousness.

Not long ago, I saw a quote from Lao Tzu: *"Stop thinking and end your problems."* Sounds simple, right? But it's really hard to just stop thinking. It's easy to get caught in your thoughts for hours, going over the same fears and worries. And I can tell you, many of those thoughts are pointless. Rather than overthink, we could spend that time doing something useful—solving real problems, reading a book, learning something new, or just resting. But instead, our minds focus on endless "What if" questions:

What if I fail?

What if I get hit by a car?

What if people think I'm a loser?

What if this? What if that?

It becomes a cycle of needless worry and fear, with no real purpose. These thoughts don't help; they just weigh us down.

Overthinking kills your happiness; peace is the price you pay for it.

Here's what I've discovered: you don't "get rid" of overthinking; you learn how to handle it.

One method is to avoid ingesting useless stuff, such as harmful thoughts, social media, or anything else that causes you discomfort. Instead, focus on what is vital and valid. Recognize your thoughts without judging yourself for them. Overthinking is not a flaw; it is simply your mind being extra careful. What counts is how you handle it. Once, I was talking to my friend, "I feel like my life is completely messed up." Why? Because I was comparing myself to others and panicking about where I was. But then I realized I was doing what I love. Yes, it is time-consuming, but I am confident that it will be worthwhile in the end.

Journaling has been quite helpful to me. My sister suggested it, and I can't thank her enough. Writing down my thoughts when I'm feeling overwhelmed has been a game-changer. Journaling reduces brain clutter and provides clarity. It's like pouring your thoughts onto paper so you can concentrate on what's genuinely important.

Thinking too much about anything hasn't solved any problems; it just leads you to a mess.

Make Choices before it's too late.

It's your choices that define your future; choose before someone else does it for you.

Chapter 12

Dopamine Effect

"The key to success is to focus our conscious mind on things we desire, not things we fear."
— Brian Tracy

You've probably heard of dopamine, the neurotransmitter in your brain that causes you to crave and seek rewards. Dopamine is what motivates you to act, whether it's eating a good meal, making new friends, or achieving a goal. It's a neurotransmitter that encourages survival activities such as eating, reproducing, and accomplishing something worthwhile.

In simple terms, dopamine motivates us to act. It raises our expectations for a prize, driving us to pursue it. This procedure has been critical to human survival throughout history. However, in today's environment, this natural process has been altered in ways that could hurt us.

Modern culture has weaponized dopamine. From junk food and alcohol to social media and addictive applications, we are continually inundated with stimuli meant to overstimulate our dopamine systems. Social media networks such as Instagram, YouTube, and Facebook are excellent examples. They are deliberately designed to attract your interest, keep you scrolling, and produce those small dopamine spikes that make you want more.

Marketers recognize the immense value of your attention. Companies spend billions of dollars generating content, notifications, and adverts to keep you engaged because the more time you spend on their platforms, the more money they gain. The problem is that much stimulation usually leaves you exhausted, distracted, and unproductive. Others become addicted to drugs, social media, or video games as a result of dopamine overproduction. The brain eventually acquires tolerance. This suggests that you will need more strong and frequent stimulation to experience the same level of pleasure. It's a vicious cycle that may hinder your ability to concentrate and enjoy simple yet crucial chores.

Your focus is one of your most valuable resources, yet it's constantly under attack. To reclaim it, start by asking yourself two simple but powerful questions:

If I stopped doing one thing today, what would most dramatically improve my focus and productivity?

What activities should I avoid to dramatically improve my capacity to concentrate?

The answers may surprise you. Many people focus on reducing screen time, avoiding needless notifications, or limiting their use of social media. Others may need to cut back on unhealthy habits such as binge-watching TV or eating too much junk food.

Good Dopamine	Bad Dopamine
Reading Books	Masturbation
Going Gym Daily	Drinking Liquor
Eating Healthy Food	Procrastination
Mastering a Skill	Sex

Dopamine isn't the enemy – it's an essential part of what drives us to grow and achieve. But when it's hijacked by overstimulation, it can derail your focus and leave you feeling unfulfilled. The key is to take control of how you engage with it.

You can prevent the dopamine trap by keeping to your routines, limiting distractions, and concentrating on truly important work. Over time, you will notice a considerable improvement in your ability to concentrate, perform well, and enjoy life's simple joys.

Consistency does mean working 24/7.

Taking breaks at several periods is also as important as working.

Chapter 13

Take a Break

"It's about consistency."
— Ryan Tannehill

I used to think consistency was about working daily no matter what the situation was, and even now, when I look around, I see people thinking the same. That's a myth. The truth is taking breaks from time to time is also as important as doing the right work. When you continuously do any work without a break, you get exhausted mentally and physically. What you can do is try to work on different things and also take naps from time to time.

The goal of boosting productivity is to labor less, not more. The goal is to complete your task in less time, allowing you to spend more time with your friends and family.

Working too long reduces your creativity and productivity. Working 12 hours is meaningless if you're not working on the right tasks. You should prioritize chores that will help you achieve your goals. Don't start climbing a ladder only to learn halfway up that it's the wrong ladder. Concentrate on your own dreams, not those of others. We should measure productivity based on the amount of work we finish rather than the amount of time we spend.

"If the ladder is not leaning against the right wall, every
step we take just gets us to the wrong place faster."
— Stephen Covey

Being mediocre is
like surrendering
in war.

When you can be extraordinary, then choose to be normal.

Chapter 14

Don't Expect

कर्मण्येवाधिकारस्ते मा फलेषु कदाचन।
मा कर्मफलहेतुर्भूर्मा ते सङ्गोऽस्त्वकर्मणि॥

Translation

Karmanyevadhikaraste Ma Phaleshu
Kadachana,
Ma Karmaphalaheturbhurma Te
Sangostvakarmani."

Meaning: "You have the right to work only but never to its fruits. Let not the fruits of action be your motive, nor let your attachment be to inaction."

I have followed Lord Krishna's teachings and learned from the great book Bhagavad Gita. The above shloka from the book Bhagavad Gita, told by Lord Krishna to warrior Arjuna in Kurukshetra (the battlefield) when he was not able to pick up his weapon and fight. He was confused between what's correct and what's wrong.

As he told Lord Krishna,"Oh, my Lord Krishna, creator of this whole, I can't do this, I can't fight." At that time, Lord Krishna said to Arjuna, "You can't control when the flower on the tree will bloom. You can only water and nurture the plant to become a tree. In the same way, you are a warrior and you are bound to follow the dharma (justice). Here, dharma is to fight as a warrior. Don't think about what will happen or who you are fighting. *Don't think about the result; you did what you had to do, and that is enough.*"

The first rule of happiness is keeping new expectations.

Our happiness depends upon our expectations more than anything else. So, in a world that tends to get better for most people most of the time, one thing is important and that is having a post to stop moving. Montesquieu wrote, "If you only wish to be happy, this could be easily accomplished, but we wish to be happier than other people and this is always difficult, for we believe others to be happier than they are." In some cases, people might become so attached to their expectations that they are unable to see the reality of a situation. This can prevent them from taking action or making decisions that would be in their best interest.

If you look into today's world, lifestyle is growing at an exponential rate. The ability to show off wealth and create envy among other people is prevalent. Here, the motivation for anyone is "I want that lifestyle which he is living." It's often hard to distinguish high expectations from motivation, and low expectations feel like giving up on your potential.

The expectation is a mind game and often drives anyone crazy. If I expect this book to be a bestseller in the first month of launch, then I won't be able to publish this book in a lifetime because I will be revolving in the loop of doubts that this is not enough. The only thing I can do is to write the best possible and take feedback from people to improve on my next book.

Being calm in
any situation is a
great weapon.

Stay calm and never lose your cool in any situation.

Chapter 15

Peace

14th January 2025, shortly before midnight. I went to bed at 9:30 p.m. because I was exhausted, but sleep was not to be found. My thoughts were racing, repeating the events of the day. A lot had happened, and I couldn't stop thinking about it.

The day began with tension and concluded with me losing my cool—an unusual occurrence, but it happened. I had a furious debate with my faculties in college, something I never imagined. My irritation had been growing all day, and during that confrontation, I snapped. I couldn't keep it inside. I stood in her cabin, looked her directly in the eyes, and said, "Fuck," before walking out. I was infuriated, uncomfortable, and overwhelmed.

Several hours later, the experience was still troubling me. I was overthinking every detail—her reaction, my outburst, and how my emotions had gotten the best of me.

"You cannot find peace by avoiding life."
— Michael Cunningham

There is just one end objective in all of this: to achieve serenity. Maintain a peaceful mentality regardless of life's challenges and events. That is the greatest prize in life. Mind mastery involves exercising control over one's thoughts. Remember that you can only attain this through consistent practice. Some people refer to it as meditation, while others use the term awareness. Avoid overcomplicating *"finding inner calm,"* regardless of the term.

Developing inner serenity doesn't require costly training.

Meditation: Mindfulness

The practice of meditation has a millennium-long history, and many contemplative techniques have their roots in Eastern traditions. The term "meditation" encompasses a wide range of methods that promote overall health, calm the mind, and synchronize the body and mind. Some types of meditation necessitate that the practitioner maintain focus on a single sensation, such as breathing, sound, image, or mantra (repeated word or phrase).

One of the other forms of meditation is mindfulness, which is maintaining attention or awareness in the here and now without passing judgment. In mindfulness meditation, we practice being aware of our breath's ins and outs and recognizing when our minds stray from the job at hand. The skill of bringing oneself back to the breath strengthens the attention and mindfulness muscles.

Mindfulness and meditation practices have the ability to enhance people's quality of life while also providing additional health benefits. Studies have examined the potential benefits of mindfulness and meditation in the treatment of pain, anxiety, stress, depression, and symptoms associated with alcoholism, nicotine withdrawal, and opiate withdrawal.

Losing your cool is not a cool thing; it affects your productivity as well as your peace.

There's a certain mindset needed to achieve growth.

You can't achieve growth with the same mediocre mindset and thinking random thoughts.

Chapter 16

The Growth

"Stay afraid, but do it anyway.
What's important is the action. You don't have
to wait to be confident. Just do it and eventually,
the confidence will follow."
— Carrie Fisher

Take Vinny Pazienza, for example. Vinny goes down as one of the best-known boxers and the triumph of resilience and the growth mindset. At the top of his career, Vinny was a boxer who got into an awful car accident, resulting in a grievous injury to the neck. The doctor said that he might never walk again, let alone step into the ring. Most would have given in at this point; Vinny didn't. Vinny, against all odds, rose to the challenge. He underwent demanding rehabilitation, ignored concerns, and learned from the mistakes along the way; some missteps kept sending him back to the starting line, but with every setback came an opportunity to learn something new about limitations versus how to rise above them. He eventually returned to the ring and even won some titles. His story epitomizes how mistakes, learning from them, and perseverance lead to incredible success.

"The more mistakes you make, the quicker you learn, and the less likely others would judge you." I have come to own this piece of wisdom over the years. Mistakes are not the end; they are but rungs on the ladder by which we rise. To grow above something, mistakes have to be committed. But another very important thing is the determination to never repeat the mistake once it is committed. This is where actual growth comes in: reflection, adjustment, and re-trying with new knowledge.

You'll find that if you encourage mistakes, they'll be made less often. Why? Because fear of perfection is replaced with the freedom to stretch, explore, make mistakes, and learn from them. Mistakes become lessons learned from practical experience rather than theory.

They make for unforgettable lessons because we live them. A growth mindset is a way of perceiving that your ability is not fixed; with sufficient effort, practice, and persistence, it can be improved or changed.

Challenges are opportunities; they should not be looked upon as impediments in life. When you adopt this mindset, mistakes no longer feel like failure; they feel like baby steps toward success.

Let's say you're learning something new. Public speaking, for example. The first time you go on stage, your mind blacks out. You forget everything you had planned to say. Your words come out jumbled because you are so flustered or nervous.

Instead of giving up, you think about what went wrong. You need some more practice, some breathing exercises, or simplified messages. Every time you do it, you get better, and soon enough, what once seemed like an ordeal becomes second nature.

Constant Learning.

Constantly updating your knowledge is very important in this fast-growing world. Learning helps you know new things and explore more opportunities, and helps you grow.

Approaching life as if you already know everything can limit opportunities for new and better experiences. If you assume you know what will happen when you attempt If you think you know what places you haven't gone to, try something new or leave space for a surprise. Consider life to be a perpetual source of learning. Your delight teaches you what is in balance. Allowing your life events to shape you can lead to personal growth and improvement.

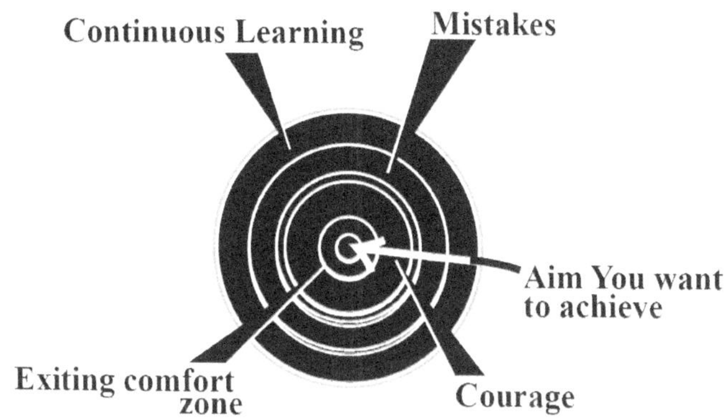

A person who has a growth mindset

- *I am still learning.*

- *I'll keep trying.*

- *I shall confront all of the challenges.*

- *I enjoy trying new things.*

- *I will learn from my mistakes.*

Learning is a way to intellectual success.

Take the Risk.

During my stock trading and financial education, I came to understand the concept of risk. Initially, I assumed that by conducting extensive study, computations, and careful preparation, I could prevent uncertainty. But the fact hit me hard: no matter how much thought or effort you put in, danger is an inevitable component of the equation. The unknown, or variable over which you have no complete control, is what puts you on edge.

In his book Same as Ever, Morgan Housel beautifully expresses this idea with the phrase, "Risk is what we don't see coming." This thought spoke to me strongly since it mirrored my own experiences. You can study from historical records, read stock reports, and listen to pundits' forecasts of the stock market, but there is always that surprise factor – the surprise announcement, the market meltdown, or the unexpected trend – that can change the game overnight.

You can't calculate risk because that is beyond your control.

Taking risks is crucial for development. We are limited to our comfort zones if it is not present. Risk encourages us to adapt, think imaginatively, and become resilient. It teaches us that failure is not the opposite of success, but rather a necessary step toward it. All the risks I have ever taken, be they successful or not, have been lessons in themselves that I would not have otherwise known. Risk must be accepted, not avoided, but recognized, embraced, and accepted. After all, all the best stories begin with a leap of faith, and all the best achievements begin from the risk. And lastly, one has to be willing to attempt even if there is no guarantee, but also not be afraid to fail. That is where real progress is.

18 Minute Rule

If you dedicate just 18 minutes each day to practicing any talent for a year, you can outperform the majority of others.

- Choose a skill. Determine the talent you wish to focus on and set precise targets.

- Schedule your practice time: Create an 18-minute space in your daily calendar.

- Reduce distractions. Find a quiet area to practice and avoid distractions.

- Practice intentionally: Focus on specific aspects of the ability that need to be improved and actively work on them.

Success cannot be Defined.

Success is a never-ending journey; at every step, you get new challenges.

Success vs Failure

Success is the sum of small efforts,
repeated day in and day out.
— Robert Collier

Choices + Learning + Consistency + Acceptance = Success

Success has never been a goal for me. It is not a finish line you cross or a trophy you display on your shelf. Every time I believe I've done something, life throws me another challenge—a higher mountain to climb, a more intricate puzzle to solve, or a deeper question to answer. For me, success is defined by progress rather than arrival.

So, *what constitutes success?*

Success is a journey. It is a thousand-mile journey of learning, achieving, growing, and advancing.

It is rising every morning with a goal, wanting to do better than the day before, and the determination to cross the line that limits you. The day you conclude you "made it," or you reached where there's no need for any further achievement, is when you stop living. Success is not just resting on the laurels. It is rather being curious and hungry for new things and, more importantly, embracing the challenges that life may offer.

If success is a journey, then failure is your map. It shows you where you've taken a wrong turn, which paths don't work, and what areas you need to explore further.

Happiness leads you to success; you can be successful and still be unhappy.

So, *what does failure mean?*

Failure isn't the opposite of success; it's a stepping stone to it. It's the universe's way of saying, "Try again, but this time, do it better." Failure is a chance to redo, refine, and master your skills. It's not a dead end—it's a detour that takes you closer to where you're meant to be.

Here's the thing about failure: it teaches you lessons that success never could. When you succeed, you celebrate. When you fail, you reflect. And in that reflection, you uncover what went wrong, what could have been done differently, and what you need to improve. Failure forces you to confront your weaknesses, sharpen your strengths, and grow in ways you never thought possible.

Success is in Choices

Two Sides of the Same Coin

Success and failure are not adversaries; they are companions along the way. If success had no failure, there would be no success. If failure had no success, there would be no failure.

Allow me to illustrate this. Consider Thomas Edison's iconic statement, *"I have not failed."* "I just discovered 10,000 ways that won't work." Every "failure" brought us one step closer to developing the light bulb. His setbacks were not failures; they were opportunities for success.

Or consider Michael Jordan, who once declared, "I've missed more than 9,000 shots in my career. I've lost almost 300 games. Twenty-six times, I've been trusted to take the game-winning shot and missed. I've failed over and over and over again in my life. And that is why I succeed."

Failure, when viewed through the proper lens, is not something to be feared. It's something to be celebrated.

Success is never-ending, and failure is your wisdom.

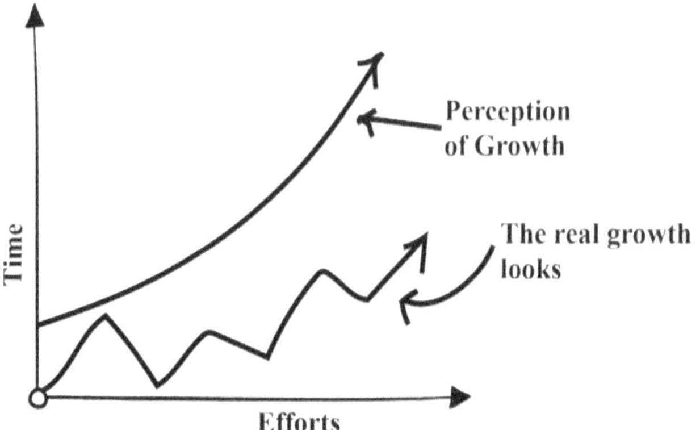

Take your
responsibility.

You are responsible for all your stuff, accept it, and have the guts to change.

Chapter 18

Own Your Sh*t

*"Accept responsibility for your life.
Know that it is you who will get you where
you want to go, no one else."*
— Les Brown

You are responsible for everything in your life, good or bad. Nobody else is accountable for where you are now. Sure, circumstances can influence you, people can guide you, and opportunities can shape your path, but your choices, actions, and mindset determine the outcome. You are the author of your story. If you want to make a difference, you have the pen. Nobody can come in and rewrite it for you.

Todd Henry once said, ***"Mediocrity doesn't just happen. It's chosen over time through small choices day by day."*** And that statement couldn't be truer.

Mediocrity isn't a sudden event or a major failure. It's the result of consistently choosing the easy path—the comfortable way out. It's letting small excuses pile up over time until you're surrounded by a life you didn't truly want.

The first thing I did when I decided to get into a better place was analyze myself, what was wrong, and how I could improve.

The first thing I did when I decided to create a better version of myself was to analyze my life deeply. I took a hard, honest look at what was wrong and asked myself tough questions: What's holding me back? What habits are keeping me stuck? What can I do to improve? Self-reflection was the starting point because, without understanding where I stood, there was no way to figure out the path forward.

I realized that change doesn't happen randomly or by chance. It all starts with self-awareness—accepting your imperfections, taking responsibility for your failures, and seeing the patterns that have been impeding your advancement. It was difficult to face these truths, but I knew that discomfort was necessary for growth. Ignoring or pretending there is no problem would just slow down my progress.

When I understood what wasn't working, I began to make actual changes. Rather than bogging myself down with big things, I broke them into infinitesimal, doable actions. If I knew I was procrastinating too much, for instance, I started with having each day's goals, no matter how inconsequential, to build momentum. If I had a bad attitude, I would do gratitude journaling and surround myself with more upbeat people.

Ask yourself three questions:

What do you want?

Why do you want it?

How far can you go for it?

Hard Choices make your life easier in the long run.

"Your work will fill a large part of your life, and the only way to be truly satisfied is to do what you believe is great work. And the only way to do great work is to love what you do. If you haven't found it yet, keep looking. Don't settle. As with all matters of the heart, you'll know when you find it."
— Steve Jobs

Say No.

"The difference between successful people and unsuccessful people is that successful people say no to almost everything."
– Warren Buffet

The distinction between successful individuals and unsuccessful individuals is that successful individuals say no to nearly everything.
– Warren Buffett

I have landed myself in trouble many times and also took on a lot of work because I had a habit of saying 'yes' to everyone. If someone asked me for assistance, I used to leave my work and go help them. After some time, I understood that this habit was leading me to the bottom; my work was pending, and people started taking me for granted.

Since then, I started practicing to say no and after that, most of the problems are solved. We tend to say yes, even if we don't want to, just because we don't want to make the other person unhappy. You agree to do everything other people want you to do, but you have limited energy and time. If you say yes to every opportunity, invitation, and task you're asked to do, you will soon begin to feel overwhelmed by it. To please others, you will lose yourself in the process. You don't have to be rude to say no. You can say it very politely; you can say, 'It will be a pleasure to assist, but please let me finish my work. Once it's done, I'll assist you.'

Your time is precious, and you have your goals and ambitions to fulfill. If you keep saying okay to everything and everyone, then your focus will be diverted, impacting your productivity. But this doesn't mean you should assist everyone and keep saying no to everyone; you should know where and when to say no.

You need to learn to say no and
set your priorities.

Things will hurt you and you will break down.

Every time you get out and try new things, it will hurt and try to bring you down.

Chapter 19

Don't Mind

"To mind, it hurts." It's a simple sentence, yet it carries a lot of weight, right? We sometimes dismiss our emotional and mental misery, believing it is less authentic or credible than physical pain. However, emotional pain may be equally crippling—it persists, festers, and changes how we perceive ourselves and the world around us.

When something hurts the mind, it's not necessarily because of what's happening in the present moment. It's because the mind has the ability to hold on to the past or brood over the future. An inconsiderate remark from someone can linger for days, a past memory can pop up and gnaw away at your serenity, and one worry for tomorrow can snowball into an avalanche of worry. Unlike wounds on the body that heal externally over time, the hurt in the mind is not linear. It comes in surprising waves, sometimes stronger than ever.

"Why do I feel this way? Shouldn't I be stronger?

"What's wrong with me? Other people have it worse."

These ideas amplify the anguish, creating a cycle in which you feel the pain while simultaneously blaming yourself for feeling it. It is exhausting. But here's the thing about the mind: it's resilient. It can mend and adapt in the same way that it feels strongly. Unprocessed emotions, unsolved conflicts, and unmet needs are common sources of mental discomfort.

To heal, you must confront these things, even if they are terrifying. It entails sitting with your sorrow rather than fleeing from it, recognizing it rather than avoiding it.

So, certainly, it hurts in the mind—but it is through pain that we learn. Through our pain, we gain clarity, strength, and a better understanding of ourselves.

Pain, as unpleasant as it is, may be a teacher if we are eager to learn. And when we do, we are transformed rather than simply cured.

Quitting and running away is for cowards.

Quitting when things get hard is the easiest thing anyone can do.

Chapter 20

Don't Quit

"It's worth risking."

When things don't seem to be working out, quitting is the simplest and most dependable option, but it provides no real growth or fulfillment. It's the way of least resistance, appealing when issues feel overwhelming. However, giving up implies accepting mediocrity, even if you have the potential to be great. Leaving will give you a temporary escape—a break from the frustration, stress, or disappointment that you experience—but in the end, you will regret it.

The reality is that everything in life is never easy. Success is always riddled with challenges, setbacks, and uncertainties. These are not signs to give up; they are lessons to be learned, obstacles to overcome, and opportunities to grow.

Every time you overcome the impulse to quit, you strengthen your resolve, learn new skills, and get closer to your goals. Success is often about persevering through pain, frustration, and numerous setbacks, but each small victory along the journey reminds you of why it is all worth it.

Giving up deprives you of the chance to find your actual potential. You like comfort more than growth, security more than challenge, and mediocrity more than greatness.

Life is too short to be safe. You owe it to yourself to keep pushing, even when it seems impossible. The pain of perseverance is temporary, but the reward of having made it through is a lifetime. Giving up is not just giving up on the goal; it is giving up on the person you would have become in difficult times.

Faith Matters.

Work to earn, but obsession with it will destroy everything.

Everyone should work to earn money because that's the ultimate goal.

Chapter 21

Money Things

"Money often costs too much."
– Ralph Waldo Emerson

One thing I learned is that you should start investing and start thinking about finances from a young age, like when you are 18 – 20 years old. It helps you understand how it works and helps you grow. Another thing I learned is that an obsession with money is also not good because it makes you greedy and destroys you.

Being in my 20s, I tried to understand the financials and stock market and how they work. Initially filled with energy, I invested some amount borrowed from my dad. Soon, I invested in it, but after some time, I lost it. I went to my dad, I said, and he laughed and told me, "You will see, money never works rapidly;

it works slowly and compounds, like success." The thing he wanted to tell is be patient; initially you will have to work to earn money but later you have to put money to work; *it's like slow and steady wins the race.*

It is very easy for money to occupy someone's mind to the extent that no rational decision is left for them, giving birth to greed and ultimately leading to disappointment.

The famous line by Warren Buffett states, ***"If you don't find a way to make money while you sleep, you will work until you die."*** It speaks of the importance of wise investments and passive income while at the same time reminding us that money is but an instrument and not the final aim. The careless pursuit of wealth has been observed to damage relationships, peace of mind, and good health.

Investment is never supposed to be a means of making money overnight but a disciplined process of building wealth over time. It is all about wise choices. As Albert Einstein said, ***"Compound interest is the eighth wonder of the world. He who understands it earns it; he who does not pays it."*** This idea applies to many aspects of life—not only money, but hard work, skill, and habit all compound positively or negatively.

Begin small, learn by doing, and be patient. Emphasize learning about healthy financial decisions, building habits, and cultivating self-discipline. Most importantly, in this scheme of things, keep your priorities set right: family, health, and happiness will always be more important than what is shown as the final figure in your bank account.

Being greedy is like gambling;
it will make or break you.

Be delusional
be obsessed.

One common thing that the top 1% of people have is that they are obsessed as hell.

Chapter 22

Productivity Secret

---

1. ***Do what you love.***

    Working on something you're passionate about keeps you motivated and makes problems feel gratifying rather than tiresome.

2. ***Avoid idiots.***

    Negative people deplete your energy and influence your mentality. Instead, surround yourself with individuals who are helpful and positive.

3. ***Stop focusing on sh*t.***

    Eliminate activities that do not correspond with your aims. This allows you to focus your time and energy on what is genuinely important.

4. ***Do it now.***

   Perfectionism and procrastination delay progress. Taking immediate action ensures momentum and helps you achieve your goals faster.

5. ***Take a Break***

   Short naps replenish your energy and increase mental clarity, allowing you to operate more efficiently when awake.

6. ***Multitasking is a myth.***

   Switching between tasks disturbs focus and reduces productivity. Instead, focus completely on one task at a time for greater results.

7. ***Journaling helps.***

   Having a clear daily schedule keeps you organized and prevents you from forgetting crucial activities. It provides a roadmap to follow, decreasing stress and increasing focus.

8. ***Timelines are important.***

   Deadlines promote urgency and accountability, ensuring that projects are finished on time rather than being postponed indefinitely.

9. ***Technological detox.***

   After spending a whole day on your laptop or phone, the best thing you can do is stay away from it. There is a 9 p.m. to 9 a.m. rule; do not use your phone or any tech from 9 p.m. at night to 9 a.m. in the morning until you feel fresher and are ready to go to work.

10. ***Do hard things first.***

This is the hard reality of life. Making difficult decisions in the short term can lead to a more comfortable life in the long run. If you want to grow, do activities you dislike that will prepare you for more difficult tasks.

11. ***Kaizen***

It entails focusing on little improvements every day rather than waiting for large changes and attempting to improve by 1% each day. Instead of creating a large goal, we should break it down into smaller goals and attack them one at a time.

**Eat healthy
Earn Wealthy
Stay Humble**

These are three simple things one can do.

Epilogue

One day, at almost midnight, I was sitting near my desk listening to music, and suddenly, I got a weird feeling: What if I was not able to accomplish what I wanted, give a good life to my family, and fulfill my dreams and goals? I was also not able to complete my bucket list. There was a weird feeling that I was getting; I felt uneasiness in my body.

But what I did was calm myself down, shut down all the tech near me, and just lay down on my bed. Then I closed my eyes and went deep inside me, and I thought, did the decisions I took give me regrets, or was I unhappy with them? The answer was NO. Then I realized my decisions weren't wrong, nor were my intentions. The only things I was not doing properly were some things, like a proper mindset and way of working toward my dreams, and from that moment, I decided to change, and a few months later, most of the things were okay. Yes, but there's a long way to go and more space to improve myself. But I am in a better place now. While writing this, I also realized a lot of things and improved a lot of things in my life, like overthinking (but I do it sometimes), but a lot has changed.

I hope that when you read this book, I will be better, and by the time you complete this book, you will also be in a better place. Just remember, the first thing you have to do before anything is BELIEVE.

BELIEVE in what you do.

BELIEVE in what you want.

BELIEVE in yourself.

And remember one thing.

*F#CK PEOPLE, F#CK THE WORLD,
F#CK YOUR THOUGHTS.*

JUST BELIEVE AND WORK TOWARD IT.

Acknowledgments

One year of writing, three years of reading and meeting, nearly four years of experience, and yet more to come. But thanks to readers, this book would be nothing without them. I hope you enjoy this book and find it helpful in changing and growing your life. My goal with each piece of material I make is to share something I wish someone else had informed me of sooner.

There's no end to growth.
Thanks for reading this book.